Broken But Not Defeated

Then the LORD answered me and said,
"Record the vision
And inscribe it on tablets,
That the one who reads it may run.
"For the vision is yet for the appointed time; it hastens toward the goal and it will not fail.
Though it tarries, wait for it;
For it will certainly come, it will not delay.

Habakkuk 2:2-3

P.O.T

I call myself P.O.T
Allow me to explain
How these on going thoughts remain trapped in my brain
I often seek silence and escape from this town
Searching high and low for any sight without sound
But there's no place in mind where I can find peace
For as long as I walk this earth these thoughts will never cease
As my thoughts talk to one another about what I don't care to know
My thoughts are like a waterfall with their on going flow
Time after time I wish these thoughts would flee
P.O.T
Prisoner of Thoughts, that's me
Still trapped in my mind with the desire to escape
If only it was all a movie with the option to rewind the tape
If it were possible I'd go for a bathroom break and never ever return

But that's not an option, my thoughts are for me to discern
I hold too much at a time with no file cabinet to place it
I hate the solution to this problem I don't wish to face it
The pain won't kill me because I've been made too strong
And because I know better, I can't do what I want in which I know is wrong
If my thoughts could be checked out of the library
I'd leave them there collecting dust
No one should want to put up with them it's too much of a fuss
I've been blessed with a gift, but at times I feel cursed
But I know God has my back, I know it could've been worse

No More Torment

What do you do when you can't…
You can't let go?
And the things you once did you just…
Just don't know
Don't know how, but you try to resist
But you're trapped in this world of tormenting bliss
Trapped in this world where you cry and cry all night
You're trying and you're trying but you know you're losing this fight
And you know you're not just hurting you, but it's so hard to flee
No matter how much I try, I know this demon is beating me!
Lord I want so bad…
so bad to conquer this
but even when I pray Father, there are thoughts of tormenting bliss.
Father what do I do, if even when I pray, I can't run?
It's like standing in almost dry cement my soul is being weighed down by a ton.
Father I can see myself with my hands reaching up to you

But there's something stopping me, and I know no more what to do.
So Lord this is me crying out, I can't take it anymore.
Lord forget knocking, I'm banging, Father please open the door!
Daddy it hurts over here. I want out.
He's hurting me.
Satin leave me alone I don't love you, LEAVE ME BE!!!
What happens when thoughts in your mind become so strong
They begin to seep into your heart?
And so you try to fight back but you're too weak to do it alone.
So you pray and you cry and scream out to God.
 Please not this again.
And you're told I got you just keep the faith.
So you're like ok I got this but yet again you feel weak.
But you ignore it because God's got it right.
I'm good.

Torment 2nd Round

I once wrote about a tormenting bliss that wouldn't escape me
Five years later it's returned stronger than ever not leaving me be
In the past I've cried for help, temporary relief would come my way
But just as sure as the oxygen we breathe, the demon would return another day
Only this time we'll call him legion, for it is many that reside in me
Day and night an on going persecution, with no intent to let me free
If one could imagine what I've allowed to take place
It's like moving in with your rapist just to save face
At times I want out, in fear of what The Lord would do to me
But I'm traveling deeper into this darkness with no available light to see
At times I cry out, but instead of for help it's for understanding
Of why this demon is a repeat offender in my life, leaving pain that's outstanding
I'm beginning to desire the unnatural again, longing to indulge in its confusion

As though my world isn't crazy enough, must I now entertain illusions?
You see I kind of stopped crying out to God for help, because He too has a breaking point
Of when he's sick and tired of being used and abused, thinking investing in you what's the point?
But they say His love is unconditional
I hope I live to see it true
But even in that we let go some times, throw in the towel, we're through
So if all is real of what I've been told, maybe I'll make it out again
And since this battle's not supposed to be mine, maybe He'll fight and win.

Breached Contract

I woke up this morning to an everlasting dusk,
In which a piece of me disintegrated to a waste pail of dust.
Beads of sweat slide down my face, as I nervously searched for a clue.
As I paced back and forth in my mind there's no sign of you.
It's like a blade so sharp causing a subtle injury,
I had not realized my loss.
It wasn't until like a ghost you were,
I then realized the cost.
The value of my smile has suddenly been removed.
The astonishing warm place in my heart has now lost its cue.
It no longer has direction, a lost traveler without a map.
Who has just come to a dead end reading,
"There's no way out You're trapped."
Leaving me feeling idle and abandoned like a horseless carriage.
I woke up this morning and realized I've just lost my marriage.

Untitled

I once heard…
It's better to have loved and lost than to never have loved at all.
I really need this thing explained to me.
It's better to have your heart broken then to have never had it pricked.
It's better to share all of you in doubt, to have it confirmed when left feeling broken and kicked.
It is better to let someone walk into your heart and leave with a piece of it torn.
Better to have opened the door for heartache, then to have never since you were born?
I'm not going to knock this love thing, for God is love, and the key He possesses.
But to claim I like the idea of losing love, a piece of my heart and possible abuse to the rest.
No, can't say I'm with that, can't say I agree at all.
If we could for a change do this the way God designed, we could for once avoid the fall.
The fall that leaves you splattered for God to clean up the mess.

The fall that leaves fear to love again, hell, at all much less.
It is better to have loved the right way, but first we must know where to start.
It is better to learn to love God, who knows what's best for your heart.
So stop settling for losing at love because you refused the rules to the game.
Stop going around playing with people's hearts and then avoiding the blame.
Now we could be a loser of love, if that's what you choose to do.
But I need to go back and study the manual, so I know when the love is true.
I won't lose at love again because I'll know how the game is played.
I'm studying the instructions that God placed here; my heart is at stake with this trade.

Who Am I

Lost with no clue of direction
And no hope for my future
Who am I?
A family cast away
Living life who knows what for today
Who am I?
Pleading for a way out
Never imagining the light of day
Who am I?
Been in and out of yearly times
No bids for second chances
You take it or leave it
Or get left behind, no time for second glances
Who am I?
I once believed I was innocent until proven guilty
That is until they proved me wrong
Locked up this time because of prior mistakes
Was told I was forgiven, but with past errors
My hope was at stake
See they'll tell me: "Only God can judge me," but that's still hard to believe
Because the blemishes on my record, supposedly God has forgiven me,

But in front of man I still plead
Pleading to be free and accepted, for who I am now
Not sure who exactly that is, but to be punished for who I was…
Is foul
If I took a guess and tried to tell you who I am;
I'd say, I'm blessed to be able to tell you today how I feel,
Blessed to be able to say those who have wronged me I didn't kill
You see I try to live by the moral right I've been taught
Regardless of others ways
Lord I pray to you this isn't it for me, and pray to see better days
Father show me I haven't been lied to
And the only one that could judge me is You
Give me back my hope, being caged in has taken it away
Father I don't know how much longer I could hold on, I'm considering giving up today

Pt. 1

A piece of my heart has been incarcerated, locked away from love
It's been judged, and frowned upon by many, attacked, pushed and shoved
Picture a heart caged in with Christ like love, understanding to say the least
But when asked to be free, it's treated as though it's a beast
They act as though it's the plague of perversion or a violent disease that kills
So I've masked my love with what's deemed normal, completely against my will
A homicide inside out, because I've hurt many along the way
Running from what felt normal to me, to be accepted another day
To be accepted for who I was openly, while stoned quietly inside
To wear shades to hide my truths while slowly within I died

Pt. 2

Take a walk with me into my truth…
You ready?
Born into sin, shaped in iniquity - with no choice in the matter
Never asked to be born, especially this way, but that doesn't even matter
From the time I observed hearts connected, this has been my story
But others would judge and count you out, unworthy of His glory
Dictate who I might love, and ridicule me when I don't
So I've pretended with wondering eyes, shared the parts of me that won't
Shared parts of me that won't allow you to love me down to my soul
Shared parts of me with reservations to hit a switch and turn cold
Revealed to you with limited sight, never allowing you to see
Hypnotizing you to fall in love not knowing all of me

Pt. 3

Tears on my pillow from the prayers never answered
Dying inside out threat worse than cancer
Studied to show myself approved - but yet to be approved
For my love is unaccepted, my soul I stand to lose
My love, my heart cries out to you, but condemned every time
He without sin cast the first stone, wait there's no one in line
For the last time my eyes have drenched this page
You're creating a monster, turned love into rage
I've loved with a Christ like love, unconditional in every measure
Instead titled perverted, immoral, like I'm in it for sexual pleasure
Disregard her cross I've bared and flood gate of tears
Or my non-stop prayers for the multitude of her fears
Love her the way Christ love the church, guess that wasn't my order

How dare I be in love with one of God's daughters
Guess not enough to believe and confess that Jesus is Lord
Because church folk have already nailed my coffin and for me shut heaven's door

Farewell

It's been a while since I've expressed pain, the original inspiration for my pen.
Leak out my tears across the paper just to keep an overflow of crying from within.
I'd write and write some more just to hold on to my sanity.
My pen has been my outlet because there's nothing but disappointment in humanity.
In silence and on going racing as usual thoughts cloud my head.
Can't seem to find my peace, faint desires to be dead.
Haven't talked to my heavenly Father in quite some time.
Not really sure what to say anymore, or if it'll be a waste of time.
Even now as the pen strokes these sheets, lost, confused, direction - no clue…
It's a constant war, lay my sword down I'm through.
Carry soul ties connected to me; give up now they'll all be done.
Name's Tashara nice to meet you, not Jesus the righteous one.
Hate to sound selfish but my strength is fading; I've lost connection to the source.

Can someone get a call up for me because behind my sin I've lost remorse?
Walking around with a: I don't give a you know what attitude...
Woke up this morning with the motto: "What Ever," might seem rude.
But the weight of the world shouldn't have to sit upon my shoulders.
I can't help but notice my heart growing colder and colder.
Becoming the very thing I hate, a vicious mind behind this smile.
If I'd known this would be me one day, I wouldn't have bore/birthed a child.
You see now responsible for a life I chose to bring in this world.
Damn can't turn back now, it's done, can't cry scared little girl.
You've made your bed now lie in it; Bite the bullet – you've fired the gun.
The war between God and satan seems over, the enemy has won.
My final destination seems fiery a burning hells pit.
You've become a wasted investment, a done deal worth spit.
Many are called, few are chosen. It's written in His word.

So you've failed test after test, your
chapter's done, last word!
So on her tombstone let it read: "A
disappointment to all, A.K.A Human,
And if done all over again she probably still
wouldn't win." 1982-2010.

Reality Check

As I look into her face I realized how much pain she held inside while her tears fell.
I asked her why she cries but she wouldn't respond.
"I've been cut by something so sharp I didn't realize it was there." She replied.
All I could do was pause. The pain she released when she said this was unimaginable.
I then asked her if she could remember, or maybe even had an idea of what caused her pain.
She looked at me and responded...
"It could have been a number of things, but here is a list of what I thought might have done it.
Just noticing the wound never realizing it was there,
Trying my best to remember what caused it.
It could've been that day I acted as a slave,
Taking lash after lash not releasing the screams of anguish
 or maybe the day...
I said yes, when all I wanted to do was rest.
 or maybe the day...

I decided to listen to the right now feeling
instead of my screaming HEART.
 or maybe the day…
When I said, no it's ok I don't mind if you
do it, knowing I wanted nothing else but to
flee from it.
 or maybe the day…
I decided to birth a child knowing I still felt
like one, and for that I'm sorry.
 or maybe the day…
I said, I do, when I really meant I don't in
every single way.
 or maybe the day…
I decided to live for me and no one else.
 or maybe the day…
I realized I never followed through with that
promise to myself after all.
 or maybe the day…"
Then I put my hand over the list and said,
Before you read any further look at me,
and as I looked back into the mirror my tears
began to pour.

Programmed for Abuse

I am so sick of missing out on all my blessings,
Because of all the built up scar tissue.
I'm sick of missing out on the good things
or letting the good one get away.
In fact I'm sick of looking for the good one.
So stop, you say?
Yeah sure tell that to the ugly scar
screaming for cocoa butter.
That tall, dark and handsome cocoa brother,
That sexy, brolic, gorgeous…
Oh wait sorry, I'm getting off track right.
I'm sick of pushing away everyone who gets
too close, or better yet…
I'm sick of letting someone get close,
Making them my world,
Then latching on like a leach.
Sucking all the life out of them with…
Shoot 50 ain't got nothing on me, 21
questions please…
Just so he can go out I need an itinerary,
And you think that's bad…
He's only been gone a half an hour
And I have to call to make sure things are
going as planned.
See this is some of what I'm sick of.

Trust me just as much as he is.
Because I know these actions are going to do the very thing that I'm trying not to.
I will lose this man faster than…
Shoot forget a punch line; this brother is gone.
So stop you stay?
I try, I swear I do. But when I don't ask, and I don't call,
My stomach gets these pains…
And my head…
Man my head…
Well my head is like Times Square before 9/11.
The clutter leaves no room for anything.
So I try making friends.
You know… to distract my mind from him.
And God, that's just another problem.
Cause now when I'm not calling him,
I'm calling them.
So now people are my drug.
So just stop you say?
But the scar tissue won't let me.
If I'm not thinking about him,
And I'm not thinking about them...
I'm thinking about my past.
Like mommy,

Mommy why weren't you there like I needed you?
Like daddy,
Daddy where were you from the ages of 3-20?
Like grandma,
Grandma why couldn't you, out live me?
Like why....?
Why is everyone leaving me,
Why wasn't anyone there when I needed them?
So people have become my drug.
I'll do anything to take my mind off the lost love.
I'll do anything...
Well...
Not anything.
I'll allow everyone to abuse me
To take my mind off the scar tissue.
Give me new pain, to cover the old pain.
Fill my heart with your problems,
So I can forget about mine.
You know what...
Never mind...
I quit it all, no more of your pain...
No more of this piece.

My Eyes My Soul

The eyes are said to be the mirror of the soul.
I wonder what all do they show.
Can anyone see my soul balled up in a knot?
Can anyone see the boiling over of my pot?
Can anyone see the fear within my heart, tucked away behind the smile?
Has anyone noticed the pain inside or are my eyes being good at denial?
Come on, look deep into them, I would love to hear what you see.
I bet you have no discernment; bet you don't know the real me.
There aren't many of you who will notice that scared little girl.
Afraid of making the generational mistakes with the child she's brought into this world.
I dare someone to get to know me; I dare you to really care.
Go ahead don't turn around now, look into my eyes as they stare.

Surrendering My Broken Heart

My eyes won't lie for me today
They just insist on telling my deepest secrets
Only they're not so deep, hidden on the surface
My smile and laughter is but shallow waters
That have began to over flow through my eyes
I'm fighting hard to camouflage these things
But that damn canary bird just insists that she sings
What bitter truths, I dare to release
For what purpose, it won't guarantee peace
One second I'm fine, or not, so it seems
Crying secret puddles into my dreams
There's much at risk if I dare to share
Too many know my past, if not would they even care
Not questioning or doubting all who love
I'm just pretty sure my history gives a shove
I know it bullies me from time to time
That is when I allow it to consume my mind
Being strong for the eyes wide shut and ears to the ground
Who couldn't hear the silent screams, or vision impaired sound

I've become a movie with subtitles for all to see
But the audio masks the narrators voice to be free
Chained and shackled… If I say one more time:
I FEEL LIKE I'M BEING HELD HOSTAGE and
No one sends in a negotiator
I can't guarantee tomorrow
Just get back into the flow of life, I tried and it won't mask my sorrow
And for those who feel like the time is still fresh
How soon before it goes stale
And please don't share your testimony of sorrow, like spirits can't heal this tale
I may sound cold to the compassion of others or hurt to say the least
I'd rather not speak at all about any of it, but it's advised that I release
Just what exactly, I really don't know
Hell when I talk about the real things, the tears begin to flow
A ticking time bomb, a rage of weakness, to mask my broken heart
I'm reaching my breaking point, towel in, flag waved

COULD MY HERO COME PLAY HIS PART?

What Do I Do

What do I do if the place I once called home
now makes my stomach turn?
What do I do if the thing I once called love
now fits perfectly in an urn?
What do I do if I want to release the pain,
but it's some how being held hostage?
What do I do if my gash is so deep it
requires more than your average stitch?
What do I do with this unfamiliar feeling, in
which I've always managed to ignore?
What do I do now when the bulldozer has
come through and completely demolished
my door?
What do I do when my heart feels
unprotected; I've been completely disarmed
of my guard?
 What do I do…?
Oh wait here is my answer,
You completely trust in God.

If Not Me Then Who

I can cry your everyday tears, you know, the broken heart caused by the world.
But what do I do at this age in life when forced back to that scared little girl?
What do I do if I've constantly been lied to?
What do I do if I'm the one telling the lies?
What do I do when I want so much to love them, but it's much easier to say goodbye?
What do I do if my promises are worth gold, to everyone, but me?
What do I do if trust is my problem when I can't even trust me?
How do I recover from heartache, in which I've caused myself?
If I can't trust me, how can I trust anyone else?
How do I live my life as a detective, when I'm the leading suspect of the crime?
What do I do if my heart has been convicted, but my soul is the one doing the time?
How is it possible that I am so trust worthy, when I am my #1 disappointment?
How is it possible for my heart to really love, if with my own heart I am not content?

The Heart Born Of A Teen

Born to a mother barely old enough to vote.
Not even her first please get the mental note.
At 18 yrs. old had two kids on her side.
This generational curse has lived long and it's live.
She never even noticed how many nights we lost sleep.
From tossing and turning, while mommy hid when she weep.
Does the best that she can so we never go without.
But who fulfills her needs, when we have food she's without.
Noticed blisters and bruises from shoes two times too small.
Just to stand all day long waiting tables as they call.
Excited over the little things, this month's bills she's able to meet.
Comes home to our smiles, clothes on our backs and shoes on our feet.
She may lack here and there, but our smiles keep her going.
Well that and God's grace, plus she goes without knowing.

That it breaks our hearts inside, when others whisper and they stare.
Instead of lending a helping hand in our time of despair.
A world with one judge only, we've yet to see the day.
Dodging daggers and stones, a bit early for judgment day.
Instead of casting the first stone, let's get the beam out your eye.
Be grateful your sins aren't walking and talking, you're still living your lie.
So the next time you pass us, keep your comments inside.
Stand in the gap for us, while we for you, for it was for All of us Christ died.

On Behalf Of The Fatherless

Abandoned… Deserted… Worthless…
These are just some of the things I felt when you picked up and left me.
Never given a real reason of what I did wrong.
Or why I was worth less than your other children you chose over me.
Wondering how you felt when you looked in the mirror
Because all I can see is your face in My reflection.
Hiding the tears behind my smile, when I would see little girls with their fathers.
Wondered how that felt time and time again.
Harboring embedded scar tissue from the scabs overlapping within my heart.
Mask the truth with men attempting to replace what I should've had from the start.
Case & Point:
One failed marriage and an engagement gone bad.
All because of a lack in balance, a mother but no dad.
And I honor her daily for the role that she played.

Yes we had our ups and downs but she manned up and stayed.
That's more than I can say for you.
A cowered if ever asked, is how I view you today.
But I do have a thank you, you deserve in the worse way.
As a single mother I could identify their pain and anger inside.
So on my face I continue to pray that they'd be better off than I.
That forgiveness would come easy for them, and trust wouldn't serve as an issue.
And God would step in early, cleaning out all pain before it becomes scar tissue.
And because of you, I picked men that wouldn't follow through.
So I pray my boys learn from God and not their fathers on what they do.
Believe me when I say, I don't hate you anymore.
Not enough love in this heart of mine to accommodate that core.
So as I let go of this pain today, I no longer hold you to blame.
I ask all of you to give it to God as I do the same.

Trust

Sometimes what might seem important, I often tend to doubt.
Just how serious it may be to release and let it out.
Talking was never my first choice until I discovered a gift.
When discussing life and my thoughts often gives others a lift.
They say: one mans trash is another mans treasure.
Maybe that's why others enjoy, my tales of life's measures.
I used to share my testimony as a way to escape the pain.
I stopped when I felt I've obtained all that I had to gain.
I noticed I've been held hostage ever since I've began to let go.
In fact an interesting choice of words because I've never completely let go.
Letting go creates vulnerability I'm not sure I'm ready to face.
Total loss of control, a lost and scary place.
I wonder if that's what has blocked my blessings, not letting go and letting God

Completely giving up on doing it myself, you wouldn't imagine how hard.
How hard it would be for me to depend completely on anyone and losing control of my life.
My Lord I've finally realized a piece of my puzzled caused strife.
Father forgive me for not really trusting You and completely giving You my life.
But I'm still not sure how to, I've held on with all my might.
For years never letting go, for fear of vulnerability.
Fears of being let down, and maybe even of defeat.
Now Father only You can teach me how to depend on You.
To let go of my fears and lay in your arms and let You do what You do.
Father help me trust You.

The Church

As I walked in church I never felt so cold
From all the pointing and mocking, from my story never told
They mocked and laughed before they even met me
And this is where I'm supposed to come to get delivered and freed
Cold glances and judgmental looks rudely awaited me
As a chill ran down my spine, my past was all I could see
They're no different from out there… who are they to judge me
At least when I see a broken heart, I know it's compassion that they need
When they fall down from all the abuse, it's an embrace I offer
Not further ridicule and torment from the heart of a mocker
Father I want to come in Your house, serve and receive my healing
But I can't take that God awful fakeness and the painful feeling
Can You please remind them in there, that He died for me too

And when they treat me this way, as I cry so do You

Know Who I Was, Before You Admire Who I Am

*Yes, before you even ask, people admire me.
You see they stand on the outside and look in,
Admiring what they see, not knowing where I've been.
I wonder how they would feel if they knew my joy, is newly found.
And the sorrow that they feel, once also had me bound.
And if they knew at one point, I too despised my mother.
Couldn't understand how the pain she had been through could affect another.
And how men would feel if they knew, I just recently began to respect them.
Before God came along, they were a game to me, in which I learned to wreck them.
Always being told "Beauty is in the eye of the be holder," never knowing what that meant.
Walked around with the lowest self-esteem never feeling love with in.
I too grew up in pain, a bastard child with no father around.*

*It wasn't that long ago when we were reunited, wasn't till then my joy was found.
My heavenly Father saved me and helped to fill the hole.
You know like that massive crater in your heart, which no one could console.
So please take note that this, "Beautiful young lady, who has it all together,"
Was not always like this.
I too had my battles to endure, to stand victorious today.
So when you're admiring the next man, just imagine what you've been through.
Remember the bigger the victory, the bigger the battle, so can you now see them in you.*

We Must Qualify

Believe it or not… I want to be led.
I want a king to guide me, protect me, make me feel safe.
Reassure me he's for me, and together we can conquer any place. I wanna know that when I'm weak, he too can pray me through.
When I'm lost and he can't help me, he'd seek God to see us through.
I need to know that I'm 1st, but second to God of course.
And a life long commitment to him, won't one day end in divorce.
So father know in my heart… I do want to submit.
But if he hasn't been uprooted, grounded and planted in You…
For me he's not legit.
I look forward to being able to follow, and confident in you leading the way.
So I need you to stand fast in God, a soldier for Him, day to day.
A soldier for God and a king for me.
United we stand; forever more we're complete.
So when submitting a resume for this job
Know the prerequisites…

~Your Lord and savior Jesus Christ
~The Holy Bible, your guide through life.
Last but not least, your objective is:
To spread love, win souls and make God look good.
God you know who's qualified and You certainly know who's not.
I'll stand by as You polish and prepare me for who ever you have got.
Just as You know my hearts desires, You too know what he awaits.
So Father I ask you that I qualify as my Boaz's help mate.

Love Melody

I remember back in the day when we were like a song.
That melody that gets stuck in your head can't help but sing along.
That song that if someone even hummed it, your heart would skip a beat.
The instrumental alone was like the orchestra of a memory.
You'd rewind the song so that thoughts would replay.
Couldn't wait to turn on the radio, her face was bound to come your way.
We were everyone's favorite tune, the sound of us made all smile.
Had both old and young generations, wishing for a love this wild.
It's crazy what music could do to you, kind of have you mesmerized.
The artist to this track was original, no plagiarism, and no lies.
We were at the top of the charts, double platinum, the highest in demand.
To this day sold out to each other, a love too strong for supply and demand.
So when you wanna hear that classic hit, be sure to tune in.

To the beat of in sync hearts, their love plays deep within.

My Best Friend

I guarantee you my best friend supersedes every friend you all have
He's there when I'm crying, wipes my tears and makes me laugh
He's my joy, my peace, my medicine when I'm sick
And since everyone else lets me down, He's the first one I'd pick
Over everyone else, I choose Him as my best friend
Because unlike the rest of you His love has no end
An unconditional love, which compares to no other
He's better than my mother, my father and the world's greatest lover
You see when I need Him; He's there, even when I don't ask
Protects me from hurt, harm and danger, forgives me for my past
Keeps a record of when I've wronged Him, but only to show how far we've come.
And while the rest of the world focuses on itself
Every battle we've fought we've won

*But I don't want to be selfish, so His love I'd
like to share
With anyone who would trust Him, to love
you the same if you dare
No longer having to wonder how I made it,
you could experience it for yourself
The love, the peace, the happiness, a life of
eternal wealth
So I'd like to extend an invitation to all
desiring a friend like no other
Accept Him while you can, Jesus Christ, my
big brother*

The Nightmare/Warning

I passed her everyday and I'd always see her crying.
In my mind I'd see me helping, saying anything to keep her from dying.
Like clock work, never failing, same corner, same time.
And I am doing the same thing over in my mind.
I'd ask her what's wrong, is there anything I could do to help?
But day after day same action, don't ask, don't tell.
She always appeared to be waiting, with a search of hope in her eyes.
If only I'd put my pride aside and stop listening to the whispering lies.
Saying no one could help her, not a bit of love will do.
I'd then hear a calm wind brush by, whispering this once was you.
A day or two went by again, I've now made up my mind to speak.
Only this time the corner's crowded, I'm pushing through at least for a peak.
There she was again, same corner and still nothing said...

If only I had spoken, she wouldn't have been laying there dead.

P.S.A.

I'm damned if I do and damned if I don't.
You see I often hated being alone, but
people's lives tormented me.
Couldn't stand being alone with my mind,
because my thoughts never ceased.
But while hanging out amongst the crowd
the gift in me never eased.
It's liked being trapped inside a big clear
box, allowed to see their pain but do nothing
about it.
It would be a short reel movie on replay:
live, hurt, die, watch the enemy get his
kicks.
So I would watch the movie one time and
write how I could relate.
Watch it again and again, while my heart
was being used as bait.
Reeled in to feel for them and pray for help
along the way.
Down on my knees and flexing my pen,
writing out the pain was the way.
You see as far as my pain thermometer
would rise, my joy thermometer would drop.
I would cry rivers with my pen and my
prayers would be the mop.

So of course I'd be a praying fool, because the West Nile would never dry up.
Calling out to God day to day about the over flowing of my cup.
I can't help but feel like we're short staff.
Too many trials and tribulations, not enough soldiers along the path.
Too many victims of hit and runs.
Not enough Bibles instead of guns.
I would like to cry out to those who feel my pain…
Sick of seeing your brothers and sisters being abused and slain.
Ready to fight for a cause, use your sword with a purpose.
Time to clamp down on the enemy, put an end to this vicious serpent.
So consider this a PSA for those of you that care.
And for those of you who don't, it is those who are in despair.
Can we join together as a nation and take back what the enemy stole from us.
It's time to stand in the gap, consider yourself the chosen ones.

If I Could Reach Just One

If I could just reach one of you, my mind would be at peace.
If I'm able to climb inside past the pain, I'd like to help it cease.
To be able to show just one, there's joy behind that wall.
To be able to reach out and help you recover from that fall.
To be able to show you, I too cry and this smile was always here.
It's just now they're tears of joy, and before a smile behind fear.
False Evidence Appearing Real once also had my mind dismantled.
Constantly trying to tell me what I can and cannot do.
How dare I hold back the victory in which set me free.
Who the hell am I to decide this joy was just for me.
So it is my D.U.T.Y and to neglect it I wouldn't dare.
To Do Unto You what was done unto me… and just simply share.
Let me reach out to one of you, to share what I know.

To be obedient to my God so you could see he'll never let you go.
When the world seemed to have turned their back on you, just go and Seek His Face.
You'll learn then, that void you've always felt; only He can fill that space.
You'll learn that, those tears you cried never knowing why.
It was God crying through you, asking how long will you deny?
Deny Him His right to love you from that pain.
For that pain wasn't yours to go through, He's your shelter from the rain.
So again I ask you Father if I could only reach just one.
Teach me exactly how to love them the way YOU would have done.

Why I Swallow Your Pain

I swallow your pain because you don't know how to.
I swallow your pain because I, I once was you.
I once was that broken spirit who lashed out at the world.
Causing my scar tissue to further deteriorate, but increasing the value of my pearl.
I swallow your pain.
You see I swallow your pain because it's your regurgitation of your past, and not yet noticed present.
If I didn't swallow your pain I would just add to it.
Causing that demon implanted fire to forever remain lit.
I swallow your pain.
I swallow your pain because I wanted someone to swallow mine.
Because had they not did it for me, standing before you now would be a waste of time.
So I swallow your pain to show you that I care.
I swallow your pain because no one else would dare.

I know exactly how it feels to have your tears out last your pain, and no one notices your hurt.
 I know how it feels to have the highest code red of suicides, but no one sees the alerts.
I swallow your pain.
I swallow your pain, digest your pain, then defecate it through my pen.
Releasing the screams of anguish that you conceal deep with in.
I swallow your pain God willingly which one day will bring you peace.
So I swallow your pain with faith that it will one day cease.

You've Heard Their Reasons, Now Hear Mine

It's because of you…
No wait because of God…
No… I got it; it's because of you, because of God.
Yes
Because of your pain God wakes me up, like now 5 o'clock in the morning
And I just gotta tell you why.
Why, I can't rest if I don't write.
How if I don't write, you don't rest.
How this gift at times can feel like a curse
Because when I wanna do anything but write, I can't stop thinking about writing.
And how when all I wanna do is write, I can't stop thinking about everything else.
So my thoughts become all jumbled up.
I end up with three pieces all in one.
And can't nobody figure out where which one begun.
I have three middles and no end.
Y?
Because pain never ends.
At least not here on this earth.
You see because down here is where all the pain began.

I can't picture down here being where this pain will end.
Just like when Adam cried out to God, "It was that woman You gave me!"
I now hear everyones cries.
So I write...
I write how Jackie is up the street trying to get her next fix,
because on the other end of that street there's her pimp who won't stop beating her.
He won't stop killing her, so she wants to help...
She wants help.
I write because of that pain that grown man is feeling because daddy never stuck around, and so now he never sticks around.
Now he has children all over but was never taught how to raise them...
So he leaves... and regrets it, every time.
So I write...
I write because she tells me to, indirectly. When she calls me crying about how he's beating her...
The way daddy beat mommy...
And all the different uncles she had would beat mommy.

And because that's all she knows she can't leave.
Because for her, this is normal.
So I write.
I write because I am sick of the dying.
Sick of the death induced by an overdose of pain.
Extra, extra read all about it…
We lost another one today.
Because the world didn't care…
Because the world didn't care, we lost another soul.
And gained another murderer.
Lost another life because the murderer overdosed on the pain from his crime.
If someone else cared besides God and the poets He placed here,
This world would be a whole lot better.
But instead no, we must write.
We must be subjected to anything we could jot a thought down on and with.
But it's not enough of that to go around.
We have more thoughts than supplies, trust me I know…
This pen, damn just ran out of ink.
But of course that doesn't matter because we've yet to run out of pain.
So we write.

And occasionally we writers want a vacation.
So we try to write something funny to vacate from the pain.
But it doesn't work, that's why out of 600 pieces
You might find ½ a funny piece.
But we try…
Try to cry for you…
Try to find someone else to care.
But until we do, we'll keep coming back
Having these annual meetings where we share.
I remember when I was quiet…
But it was never quiet, I heard voices,
And stories, and crying and never could make it stop…
Then I heard a poem.
I thought, so this is what you do with these thoughts…
So I write.
I write for every time my little boy asks,
"Mommy why doesn't she like me, I said hi and she didn't speak back?"
I tell him, sweetie it's not that they don't like you,
It's just everyone isn't as kind as you.
Then I write…

*God I wish people cared the way you care.
The way an innocent child cares before they're corrupted.
Lord I would do anything just to be able to help...
These were my prayers, and do you know what He told me to do?
To WRITE!!!*

I Broke Out Of Prison With My Pen

Trapped behind the bars of pain
With no bail or trial to arraign
Sentenced to life with no chance of parole
Told it'll be a cold day in hell before we let you go
Bound to nothing but generational curses
Watched my family's soul ties lead us into hearses
I'm imprisoned by my pain
But used my pen to do the slaying
I couldn't be convicted of escape, because I really went for an appeal
Tried and tried but kept getting denied, fate classified, case sealed
You'll never make it out of here alive, is what they tried to tell me
But my heart wouldn't let me believe it, just knew my pen would be the key
Father God You've blessed me to write, so I'll write these prayers to You
You said You'll never leave or forsake me, so I look to You for the truth
No weapon formed against me shall prosper, I hold You at Your word
So I know these attacks of the enemy can't stop me from soaring like a bird

So as I stand on Your word, I let out my pain to keep from being bitter
And no matter what wrongs life has dealt me, I remember to forgive her
We must forgive to be forgiven, remember Love is key
And if you can't talk, use your pen to write, it always worked for me
Don't let anyone else; especially the enemy determine who you are
As for me and my prayers, faith and my pen helped to break my bars

My Calling I Will Do

You are the cause of this world's happiness.
Every smile blessed upon our faces is
because of Your righteousness.
You bring joy and grace to everyone's life.
But they can't all see it because of their
strife.
We allow the little things to come between
Your greatness.
And it's those little things that tend to make
us depressed.
We struggle day by day going through our
journeys.
Trying to live saved so our souls will remain
free.
I become aggravated when I feel there is no
way out.
I begin to pray for You to show me You are
there without a doubt.
It's not that hard to notice You standing
right before my face.
If I just stop running around You, to keep up
with the others pace.
I begin to turn around to the voice behind
me, but I don't see anyone.
"My child you must **not** follow those who
do wrong,

Make them follow you, lead them to be strong."
I realize what You're saying, but scared to take on that responsibility.
You want me to lead Your children, show them what it means to be free.
I will do what I've been told; I know exactly where to start.
I will bring Your children to You; You will no longer be apart.

Broken But Not Defeated

I've traveled life's journey, been beat down to bloody bones
Stripped of my self-esteem, broken with no will of my own
Torn of my will to fight, stripped of my love of self
Told I would never amount to anything, my soul would be my wealth
Buried the demons that haunted me, deep within my flesh
Endured their cannibalism from inside to out, many nights with no rest
Cried for a way out, wept for some compassion
Until God stepped in and informed me, *All It Took Was Me Asking*
He cured and mended my heart of all loss and pain
May have been broken but never defeated, my victory I had gained

The Beauty of a Woman

Curves so deliberate to fit her perfect mind
With each one being different, made one of a kind
Made so beautifully with so much we hold
He created us all equal and in a perfect mold
No other creature can hold our heart
No one can ever copy us; we're a masterpiece in art
No man can come close or imagine the things we know
I believe he made us stronger, with an unbreakable soul
A woman can carry her cross with room to help another
We were put here for a purpose; we're here to help our brother
There is a lot we could hold before we start to complain
The Lord made us this way, if men they'd go insane
I thank the Lord personally for my blessings built within
If I had the choice to be made all over, please make me the same again

www.ingramcontent.com/pod-product-compliance
Lightning Source LLC
Chambersburg PA
CBHW070106100426
42743CB00012B/2657